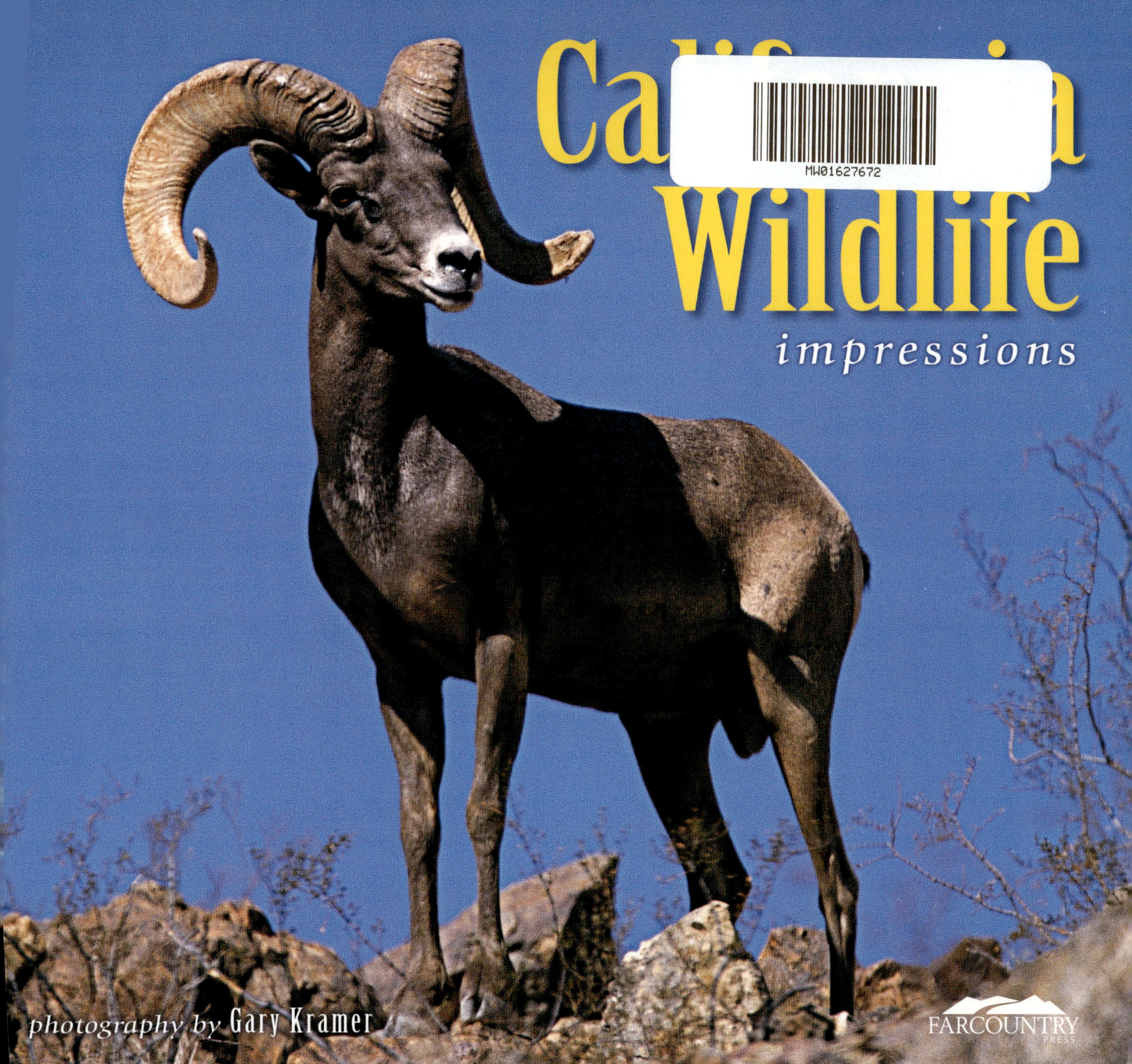
Wildlife
impressions
photography by Gary Kramer
FARCOUNTRY PRESS

FRONT COVER: Red foxes are native to the Golden State's Sierra Nevada but were introduced to the Central Valley and to southern California.

BACK COVER: This pronghorn doe and fawn survey their territory from a rocky ridge. Pronghorns are found in the sagebrush regions of northeastern California.

TITLE PAGE: Well adapted to an arid environment, this desert bighorn sheep ram watches over his domain in southeastern California.

RIGHT: Sea otters frequently float on their backs to rest, preen, and eat. Protected under the Marine Mammal Protection Act, otters inhabit the central coast.

ISBN 10: 1-56037-398-9
ISBN 13: 978-1-56037-398-8

Text by Gary Kramer

For more information about our books write Farcountry Press, P.O. Box 5630, Helena, MT 59604; call (800) 821-3874; or visit www.farcountrypress.com.

Created, produced, and designed in the United States.
Printed in China.

10 09 08 07 06 1 2 3 4 5

Introduction

by Gary Kramer

The expanse of land stretching from Oregon to Mexico and from the Pacific Ocean to the eastern slope of the Sierra Nevada covers 163,707 square miles. Named California by early Spanish explorers, the Golden State is 770 miles long and 250 miles wide, making it the third largest of the nation's fifty states. It is home to 14,494-foot Mount Whitney, the highest peak in the continental United States; and Death Valley, the nation's lowest point, at 282 feet below sea level. In between are some of the most varied habitats on the globe, including alpine meadows, towering redwood forests, vast grasslands, coastal estuaries, ocean waters, inland marshes, immense rivers, and fiery deserts. California is home of the sprawling urban areas of Los Angeles and San Francisco, the most productive agricultural lands in North America, and expanses of rangeland where livestock still outnumber people.

The wildlife of the Golden State is as varied as the habitat. Some species, such as sea otters, harbor seals, and California sea lions, reside in or make their homes in marine environments. Others, including desert bighorn sheep, antelope squirrels, and roadrunners, prefer hot desert environments. In contrast, Merriam chipmunks, black bears, and porcupines are found in the mountains where the air is thin and winters are long.

Ospreys feed on fish and can be found near lakes, reservoirs, rivers, and in coastal regions. They build a large conspicuous nest of sticks.

The Central Valley, a vast grassland that has been largely converted to farmland, is in the center of the state. Drained by two massive rivers that flow to the Pacific Ocean, the San Joaquin Valley in the south and Sacramento Valley in the north support large concentrations of migratory waterfowl, shorebirds, and passerine birds, as well as an impressive array of mammals, reptiles, and amphibians.

Even the urban areas, particularly those adjacent to undeveloped lands, provide habitats for increasing populations of wildlife, including wily coyotes, mischievous raccoons, elusive mountain lions, an array of backyard birds, and even rattlesnakes.

California is rich in avian fauna, with more than 640 species recorded. These include widespread birds such as California quail and great horned owls, species tied to marine environments such as brown pelicans and black oystercatchers, wetland birds including snow geese and white-faced ibises, and species found in the mountains and foothills such as Stellar's jays and endangered California condors.

California also hosts an impressive array of mammals ranging from tiny water shrews to regal mule deer to the true giants of the animal world—blue whales and California gray whales. Among the mammals are Tule elk, a subspecies of elk found only in California that at one time numbered less than fifty animals. Today, their populations have expanded significantly, as have the populations of introduced Rocky Mountain elk in the northern mountains and native Roosevelt's elk on the northwestern coast.

An interesting group of reptiles and amphibians inhabit California's varied habitats, including the tiger salamanders and western pond turtles of the interior wetlands, chuckwallas and western diamondback rattlesnakes of the dry desert areas, and the widespread California king snakes and gopher snakes.

A search for wildlife in the Golden State boasts a cornucopia of species. Because of the varied climates, elevations, and habitats, California has the largest diversity of wildlife of any similar-size region in North America. Some species, such as bald eagles, are found throughout the United States; others, such as black-tailed deer, are found only in the West; and still others, including dolphins and porpoises, are found only in marine environments. A few—Tule elk, California condors, and tri-colored blackbirds—are native only to California.

In the process of gathering photographs for this book, I traveled the state's back roads and highways from the temperate rainforests of the north coast to the Joshua tree-studded deserts of southeastern California and from the Pacific Ocean to the Sierra Nevada. Along the way, I photographed magnificent Roosevelt's elk and massive elephant seals during breeding season, flocks of waterfowl and passerine birds during fall migration, and raccoons and mink as they foraged along mountain streams.

I have seen wildlife that is varied and unique—in national parks such as Yosemite, national wildlife refuges such as Sacramento, state parks such as Anza Borrego, and in my own backyard—all within the boundaries of the jewel of the West called California.

The last wild California condor was captured in 1987. However, through captive breeding programs, the birds have been reintroduced into the foothills and mountains of southern and central California.

LEFT: Barn owls are common throughout the state in places where there are mice and rats and suitable nesting areas such as barns, abandoned buildings, tree cavities, and caves.

FAR LEFT: A young black-tailed jackrabbit, or hare, rests on a carpet of spring flowers. In contrast to rabbits, which are born naked and with closed eyes, young hares are fully furred and have open eyes at birth.

BELOW: The venomous western diamondback rattlesnake warns intruders to stay away by making a distinctive buzzing noise with its tail rattle.

RIGHT: Two harbor seals, which are a widespread species along the coast, interact near Moss Landing.

BELOW: A large lizard of the southeastern deserts, the chuckwalla is an herbivore that eats leaves, buds, flowers, and fruit.

LEFT: The swollen neck and curled lip of this black-tailed deer buck are signs that the breeding season, or rut, is in full swing. The rut typically takes place between September and November, varying by region.

BELOW LEFT: The greater roadrunner feeds on small snakes, lizards, and mice in the arid regions of central and southern California.

BELOW RIGHT: The most widespread rabbit in the Golden State, the desert cottontail is characterized by its large ears and small body size.

ABOVE: California ground squirrels are widespread throughout the state except in the high mountains and southeastern deserts.

FACING PAGE: The yellow-bellied marmot is a large rodent found in rocky areas at elevations of up to 12,000 feet, principally in the northern and eastern portions of the state.

LEFT: Deer are the primary prey of the widespread but secretive mountain lion (also known as the cougar or puma). Adult males weigh up to 150 pounds; females average 90 to 100 pounds.

BELOW: Red-eared turtles, introduced as escaped or released pets, are now found throughout the warmer areas of California.

RIGHT: These two- to three-week-old Canada goose goslings have found a warm place to rest.

FAR RIGHT: Black bears are found throughout the mountains, where they feed on berries, tubers, grass, small mammals, and carrion. At times they can become a nuisance, particularly in national parks and forests where they are known to raid garbage cans and campsites.

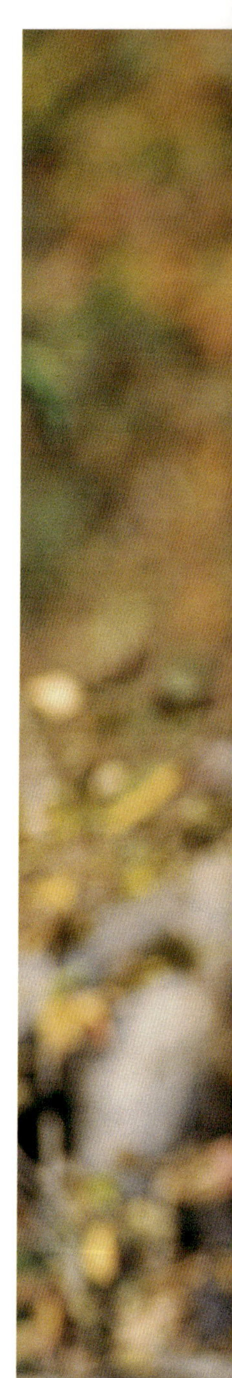

FACING PAGE: This short-tailed weasel, or ermine, is a creature of the northern mountains. In the late fall, its brown fur of summer turns white except for the black-tipped tail. In places where snowfall is minimal, its coat stays brown, even in winter.

BELOW: The Pacific Flyway population of lesser snow geese breed in Canada's Arctic and on Russia's Wrangel Island and winter in the Central Valley. They migrate through the Klamath Basin in the spring, often when there is still snow on the ground.

RIGHT: Most frequently seen in marine waters from the San Francisco Bay to the Mexican border, brown pelicans nest on offshore islands. They rarely venture inland, except to the Salton Sea.

FAR RIGHT: A pair of American wigeons at the Sacramento National Wildlife Refuge.

LEFT: Similar in appearance to the larger gray fox, the island fox is an endangered species found only on the Channel Islands off the southern California coast.

FAR LEFT: Found in habitats ranging from deserts to alpine meadows, badgers are burrowing animals that prey on gophers, ground squirrels, chipmunks, and other small mammals.

RIGHT: Weighing up to seventy-five pounds, the beaver is the largest rodent in North America.

BELOW: The native western pond turtle was a widespread species, except in desert and high mountain regions, but its numbers have declined in recent years.

LEFT: A western tanager is caught in the act of looking for nectar in a flowering bottle brush tree.

FACING PAGE: A common bird in the Golden State, this house finch pauses for a moment atop a spray of spring redbud blossoms near Paso Robles.

BELOW: White-crowned sparrows spend the fall, winter, and early spring in California and then migrate as far north as Alaska to breed.

RIGHT: In December and January, gray whales can be seen off the coast on their 6,000-mile journey from the northern Pacific and Arctic oceans to their breeding grounds in the lagoons of Mexico. PHOTO BY BRANDON COLE

BELOW: The Pacific white-sided dolphin is an offshore species that often travels in schools of hundreds, if not thousands. PHOTO BY BRANDON COLE

FACING PAGE: Black bears have several color phases. Here black- and cinnamon-phase bears pause after a spring snow squall.

BELOW: The sleek and graceful river otter is at home on land and in the water, where they hunt for fish, frogs, turtles, and crayfish.

RIGHT: Both male and female desert bighorn sheep have horns, but the rams' curved horns are the larger of the two.

BELOW: A bird of the West, prairie falcons hunt for birds and small mammals in deserts, plains, and grasslands.

FACING PAGE: A striped skunk searches for insects in a carpet of fall leaves.

BELOW LEFT: Killdeer nest in open areas, laying a clutch of four mottled eggs.

BELOW RIGHT: American avocets nest in open areas near wetlands, where they lay four eggs in a simple depression often lined with sticks.

RIGHT: A magnificent Rocky Mountain bull elk stands on a grassy ridge. Rocky Mountain elk were introduced into the Mount Shasta area in the early 1900s.

FACING PAGE: The ubiquitous gray fox is fond of climbing trees and feeds on small mammals, birds, insects, and plants, particularly the berries of manzanita and toyon bushes.

RIGHT: A male American goldfinch sits atop a blooming thistle.

FAR RIGHT: The male wood duck is one of the most striking of all waterfowl. Although the birds are distributed throughout the state, the largest populations are in the Central Valley.

LEFT: One of the largest winter concentrations of bald eagles in the continental United States is found in the Klamath Basin on the border of California and Oregon.

FACING PAGE: Rocky Mountain mule deer are found in the Great Basin of northeastern California, where the climate features four distinct seasons.

BELOW: Mountain cottontail rabbits inhabit the sagebrush and rocky areas in the state's northeastern regions and in the Sierra Nevada.

RIGHT: The semi-aquatic mink is found near wetlands, streams, rivers, and lakes in the state's northern and central regions, where they forage on fish, crayfish, small rodents, and birds.

BELOW: The white-tailed antelope squirrel is a small burrowing rodent that lives in the eastern desert washes and plateaus.

FACING PAGE: Still growing, the antlers of these black-tailed deer bucks are covered in velvet. In early fall, the velvet will be rubbed off and hard antlers will appear in time for the breeding season.

BELOW: Several Canada goose families have banned together to form a "gang brood."

Red foxes cope with cold winter temperatures by growing a luxurious coat of fur.

RIGHT: The bobcat is found from below sea level in Death Valley to above timberline in the Sierra Nevada. A fierce predator, its main prey are rabbits and small rodents, although it has been known to kill deer, particularly during the winter.

BELOW: The coyote is the most widespread predator in California and can be found from the suburbs of Los Angeles to the remote plateaus of the northeast.

RIGHT: The largest of the quail species, mountain quail have a distinctive, straight top-knot.

FAR RIGHT: The most common and widespread species of waterfowl in North America, mallards can winter in areas where most lakes and wetlands freeze, provided they have a food source and secure resting areas.

ABOVE: Found in the western portion of the state, opossums are nocturnal animals and the only marsupials in North America. The young, born in litters of ten to fourteen, are small enough at birth to fit in a teaspoon.

LEFT: Porcupines are large rodents that are more at home in trees than on the ground. They are best known for their sharp quills, an effective defense against predators.

Fishers are secretive animals of the Sierra Nevada and the northern Coast Range that prey on squirrels, rabbits, and birds. Fishers are one of the few animals that can kill porcupines.

BELOW: Long-billed curlews are large shorebirds that winter along the coast and in the wetlands and grasslands of the Central Valley.

ABOVE: The widespread black-crowned night heron feeds on small fish, frogs, and crayfish, primarily at night.

RIGHT: These northern elephant seals are located at Año Nuevo State Reserve, home of the world's largest mainland breeding colony of northern elephant seals. They come ashore between December and March for the breeding season, and bulls weighing up to 5,000 pounds gather a harem of nearly a dozen cows.

LEFT: Burrowing owls, as their name implies, live in burrows in the central and southern regions, where they feed on insects, small mammals, and reptiles. Although they are widespread, their populations have declined because of agricultural expansion and urbanization.

FAR LEFT: By the 1870s, the once-abundant populations of Tule elk had declined to fifty animals. Protection of the animals in wildlife reserves and relocation to former habitats has significantly increased their numbers.

RIGHT: A flock of long-billed dowitchers flies over a coastal wetland.

BELOW: Sandhill cranes nest in the northeast and winter in the Central Valley, where they roost in wetlands and feed in grain fields and on grasslands.

LEFT: The tarantula is the largest spider in North America and is found throughout the state's drier regions. While venomous, it seldom bites unless provoked and is no more dangerous to people than a bee or wasp sting.

FACING PAGE: Feral pigs, or wild hogs, are found in the Coast Range and Sierra foothills and are descendants of domestic pigs and true European wild pigs. The first European wild pigs were released in Monterey County in 1925.

BELOW: The widespread California king snake preys on rats, mice, and other small rodents and has been known to kill and consume rattlesnakes.

FACING PAGE: A magnificent Rocky Mountain mule deer buck stands stock still at Lava Beds National Monument.

BELOW: A pair of California thrashers feeds along the edge of a desert water hole.

ABOVE: Absent only from the driest deserts, the raccoon occupies the role of the medium-sized omnivore in the food web.

LEFT: A California sea lion shares its rocky perch in Monterey Bay with Heermann's gulls. During the breeding season, California sea lions are found from the Channel Islands to the Mexican border; in winter they can be found along the entire coast.

FACING PAGE: Greater sage grouse are found in sagebrush habitats in the state's northeastern and eastern areas. Each spring, males gather on dancing grounds, known as leks, where they display to attract females.

BELOW LEFT: When gold was discovered at Sutter's Mill in 1848, there were no wild turkeys in California; they were first introduced in the late 1800s. It was not until the 1950s that their range began to expand to many regions of the state.

BELOW RIGHT: Native to Asia, ring-necked pheasants were first introduced in California in 1889. Today, they are a widespread game bird often found in agricultural regions, particularly in the Central Valley.

ABOVE LEFT: This handsome male California quail, the state bird, perches on an old fence at Point Reyes National Seashore.

ABOVE RIGHT: During the breeding season, common snipes are found near meadows and wetlands in the northeastern and eastern portions of the state, where males frequently sing from fence posts to attract mates.

FACING PAGE: The ash-throated flycatcher is a common breeder that migrates to Mexico to spend the winter.

RIGHT: Absent only from the North Coast and the higher elevations of the Sierra Nevada, black-tailed jackrabbits can survive on limited water and desert vegetation.

BELOW: The California toad is found throughout the state, except in the southeastern deserts.

ABOVE: Wild or feral horses, including this mare and colt in Inyo County, can be found in regions such as the Great Basin.

LEFT: Anza-Borrego Desert State Park is one of the best locations to spot desert bighorn sheep, such as this adult ram and ewe.

LEFT: The California tiger salamander is found west of the Sierra Nevada between Sonoma and Santa Barbara counties.

FACING PAGE: A great egret captures an earthworm in the Grasslands Ecological Area of Merced County.

BELOW: The bullfrog is the largest frog in North America. Its diet includes insects, minnows, other frogs, and crayfish, but it has been known to capture and consume small snakes, mice, and birds.

LEFT: The western meadowlark is often seen in California's grasslands. In spring, males perch on fence posts and sing to attract mates.

FAR LEFT: A black-tailed deer fawn pauses in a meadow of yellow flowers.

ABOVE: The great horned owl is found in areas ranging from the coastline to the mountains, and it is a fierce avian predator, preying on rodents, rabbits, and other mammals, including skunks.

RIGHT: These great horned owlets in the Central Valley have left their nest, but they are still dependent on their parents for food.

RIGHT: A great blue heron rests on the edge of the Salton Sea at sunset.

FAR RIGHT: Roosevelt's elk on a ridge at sunset, Redwood National Park.

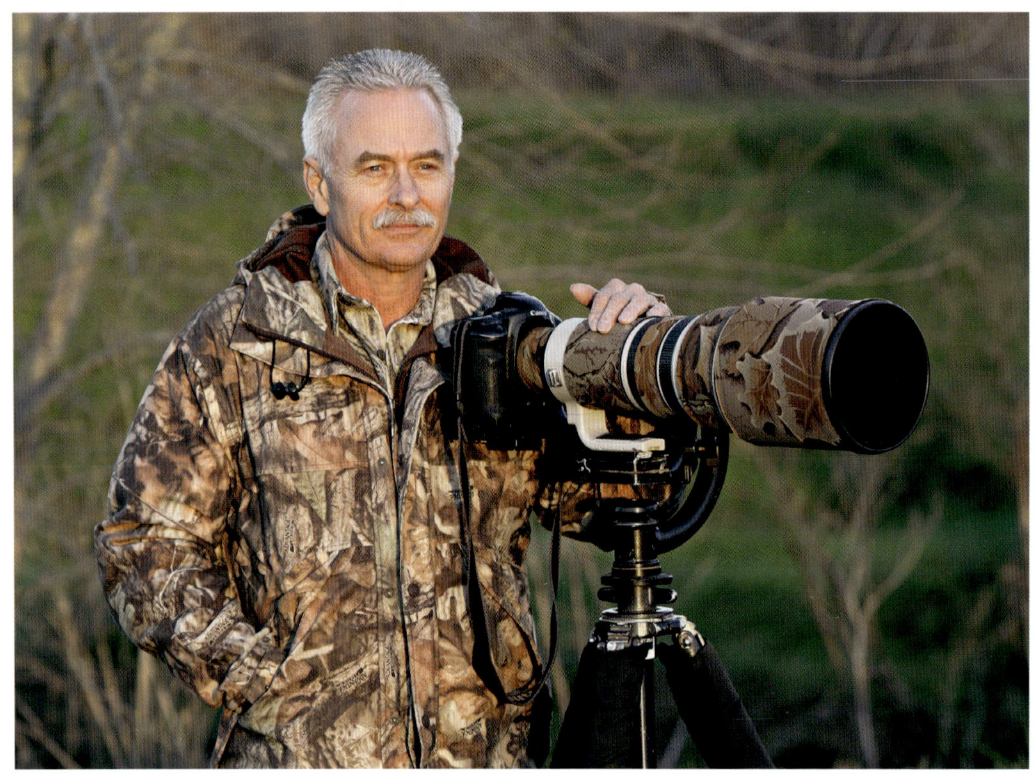

A California native, Gary Kramer graduated from Humboldt State University with undergraduate and graduate degrees in wildlife management, and then he embarked on a twenty-six year career with the U.S. Fish and Wildlife Service. Gary was a biologist at the Kern and San Luis National Wildlife Refuges in California and was the refuge manager of Salton Sea and Sacramento National Wildlife Refuge Complexes. He retired in 1999 to pursue wildlife photography and writing full time.

Gary is a contributing photographer for *Sports Afield* and his writing and photography appear regularly in *Ducks Unlimited* magazine, *Outdoor Life, Birder's World, Wild Bird,* and many other magazines, books, and calendars. This is the fourth book Gary has written and photographed. To see more of his work, log on to www.garykramer.net.